BUILDING A NEW WORLD

BY JIM OLLHOFF

VISIT US AT
WWW.ABDOPUBLISHING.COM

Published by ABDO Publishing Company, 8000 West 78th Street, Suite 310, Edina, MN 55439. Copyright ©2012 by Abdo Consulting Group, Inc. International copyrights reserved in all countries. No part of this book may be reproduced in any form without written permission from the publisher. ABDO & Daughters™ is a trademark and logo of ABDO Publishing Company.

Printed in the United States of America, North Mankato, Minnesota.
042011
092011

 PRINTED ON RECYCLED PAPER

Editor: John Hamilton
Graphic Design: Sue Hamilton
Cover Design: Neil Klinepier
Cover Photo: Alamy
Interior Photos and Illustrations: Alamy-pgs 22, 23, 28 & 29; AP-pgs 6, 7, 9, 12, 13, 14, 15, 19 (map), 20, 21, 24 & 25; Corbis-pgs 18, 19, 26 & 27; iStockphoto-pgs 8, 10 & 11; Granger Collection-pgs 16 & 17; National Geographic-pgs 4 & 5.

Library of Congress Cataloging-in-Publication Data

Ollhoff, Jim, 1959-
  Building a new world / Jim Ollhoff.
    p. cm. -- (Hispanic American history)
  Includes index.
  ISBN 978-1-61783-053-2
  1. America--Discovery and exploration--Spanish--Juvenile literature. 2. Spain--Colonies--America--History--Juvenile literature. 3. Explorers--America--History--Juvenile literature. 4. Explorers--Spain--History--Juvenile literature. 5. Spaniards--America--History--Juvenile literature. I. Title.
  E123.O45 2012
  970.01'6--dc22
                         2011012348

CONTENTS

Building a New World 4

Settling in New Places 8

Puerto Rico and the Caribbean Islands 10

Florida 12

New Mexico and Arizona 16

Texas 21

California 22

Spanish Settlement of Other Areas 26

Glossary 30

Index 32

BUILDING A NEW WORLD

Why did Spain want to settle in the New World? At first, the Spanish were looking for a way to get to Asia. Spain wanted to set up trading with the eastern countries, and was trying to find a good way to get there. When Christopher Columbus landed in the Caribbean islands, he at first thought he had found Asia.

It quickly became clear that this land mass wasn't Asia. Instead, it was a continent unknown to the Europeans. They began to view this New World as an obstacle, and started looking for a water passage through it to Asia. This fabled waterway, dubbed the Northwest Passage, was never discovered. (People eventually built a waterway. The Panama Canal opened in 1914, creating a water route from the Atlantic Ocean to the Pacific Ocean.)

Although it was seen as an obstacle at first, the Spanish soon realized that the New World offered many resources that Asia didn't have. They began to see that the Americas held promise and opportunity. So, the Spanish began searching for resources that they could bring back to Spain. The best resource was gold. Spain was desperate for gold, since it was spending so much money on wars in Europe. Another important resource was silver.

The *Santa Maria,* Columbus's largest ship, ran aground off Hispaniola, today's Haiti and Dominican Republic. It was abandoned there.

5

As time went on, the Spanish also began to see the New World as a place to live. Farms and ranches began to spring up, and people filled the towns and cities.

Another reason that the Spanish wanted to settle the New World was to Christianize the American Indians. The conquistadors brought priests with them to help turn the Indians to the Catholic faith. However, the Spanish often used force to convert the Indians. For example, they sometimes marched villagers into rivers at sword point, and then baptized them all at once. Some Catholic priests spoke out against abuse and corruption, but many priests participated in the forced conversion and abuse of the native Indians.

Conquistadors destroy an idol.

SETTLING IN NEW PLACES

When the Spanish settled into the Americas, they brought their culture with them. They founded many cities and towns. Cities such as Los Angeles, Santa Fe, and San Antonio still bear their Spanish names.

The Spanish brought a particular kind of architecture and city planning, too. Buildings were constructed with adobe bricks, which are made of sand, water, and clay, and then dried in the sun. Roofs were made of tiles, and buildings were often decorated with beautiful mosaics.

The Spanish colonizers were mostly men. They often married Indian women. This Spanish-Indian marriage was not only tolerated, it was encouraged. The majority of Latino people today can trace their roots back to both Spanish and Indian ancestors.

The colonizers started in the Caribbean islands, and South and Central America. From bases in those areas, they then colonized Florida, New Mexico, Arizona, Texas, and California.

The Mission San Juan Capistrano in California was built of adobe bricks in the 1700s.

Spanish settlers colonized the North American areas of Florida, New Mexico, Arizona, Texas, and California.

PUERTO RICO AND THE CARIBBEAN ISLANDS

To protect themselves from natives, as well as English, French, and Dutch raiders, the Spanish built large forts. In the 1500s, Fort San Felipe del Morro was built near San Juan Harbor in Puerto Rico. It stands today.

Christopher Columbus landed in the islands of the Bahamas on October 12, 1492. Some historians say he landed on the island of San Salvador. Others say he landed on the island of Samana Cay. From there, he explored Cuba and Hispaniola (today's Haiti and Dominican Republic). He believed that he had landed near Asia, and continued to believe that until his death in 1506.

Within a few years of Columbus's landfall, the Spanish royalty began to send colonizers and military troops to the New World. They landed in Hispaniola, Cuba, Puerto Rico, and other islands. They subdued the local Indian nations, often killing or enslaving large numbers of them.

The Spanish began to build large forts on several of the islands. These forts, many of which are still standing today, provided protection for the colonists. The forts provided refuge from pirates, and from English and Dutch navy ships.

FLORIDA

The conquistador Juan Ponce de León received permission from Spain to explore lands to the north of Cuba.

Ponce de León landed on what he believed was a large island. It was the Spanish custom to name new lands according to the church year. Since it was the Easter season, or *Pascua Florida* ("The Festival of Flowers") in Spanish, and because he saw many flowers along the shore, de León named the new land "Florida."

Ponce de León claimed the land for Spain, even though there were several Native American nations living on the land. The Native Americans drove off the Spanish, but de León returned in 1521. He wanted to conquer the Native Americans and colonize the land. However, the Spanish were driven off again, and Ponce de León was fatally wounded in the battle.

Ponce de León was fatally wounded in battle.

Other Spanish expeditions explored the land in the years to come. Other European countries, such as France, also wanted to colonize Florida. In 1565, the King of Spain decided that Florida must be colonized in order to keep it out of the hands of the French. He sent Admiral Pedro Menéndez de Avilés, with a large group of soldiers, to begin to secure Florida. One of the areas he took was a French settlement, which he named St. Augustine. The city of St. Augustine is the oldest continuously inhabited city in the United States. It was inhabited more than 50 years before the English settled at Jamestown, Virginia.

Spanish Jesuit priests, and then Franciscan monks, began to serve as missionaries to the American Indian nations. The Spanish missions spread, and more places in Florida were colonized.

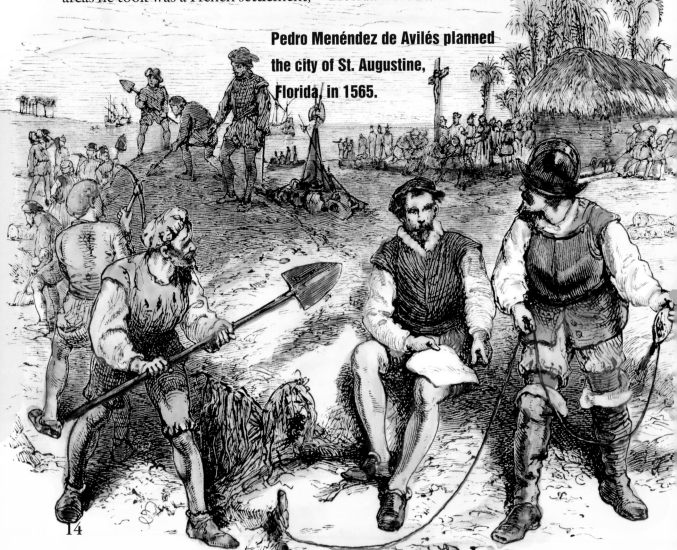

Pedro Menéndez de Avilés planned the city of St. Augustine, Florida, in 1565.

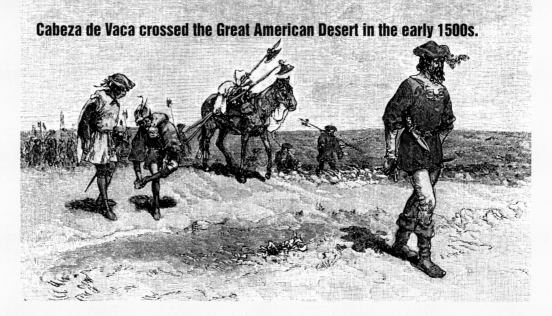

Cabeza de Vaca crossed the Great American Desert in the early 1500s.

Cabeza de Vaca

In 1527, six hundred soldiers led by Pánfilo de Nárvaez attempted an expedition to Florida. However, a hurricane blew them off course, and they were shipwrecked near today's Tampa Bay, Florida. Their boats were destroyed, they had no food, and they were attacked by American Indians.

They knew they needed to make it back to Mexico City, but it was a long journey. They traveled through Mississippi, Texas, and probably New Mexico and Arizona. Finally, in 1536, they made it to the Pacific Ocean. From there,

they went south to Mexico City. They endured poverty, hardships, battles, lack of food, and enslavement by American Indians. By the time they made it to Mexico City, only five men were still alive.

One of the survivors was Álvar Núñez Cabeza de Vaca. He returned to Spain and wrote a history of his journey. He had become friends with many Native Americans, and was a skilled trader and diplomat. Unlike other explorers of his time, he developed a great respect for the American Indian nations, and promoted friendly relations with them.

NEW MEXICO AND ARIZONA

Coronado searched for gold in the American Southwest.

In 1540, Spanish conquistador Francisco Vásquez de Coronado led a huge expedition of more than 1,000 men into what is now Arizona and New Mexico. He also traveled through northern Texas and as far north as Kansas. He was looking for the legendary Seven Cities of Gold. These were cities that were rumored to have more gold than the Aztecs or Incas. Of course, there was no such place as the Seven Cities of Gold. However, Coronado explored a large part of the American Southwest, including the Grand Canyon and the Colorado River.

Coronado claimed for Spain the land that he explored, even though there were several Indian nations living there. The first governor of the land, called New Mexico, was Don Juan de Oñate. He established a capital in 1598 north of today's Santa Fe, New Mexico.

A few years later, the capital was moved to Santa Fe. Missionaries and soldiers in the new city tried to convert and conquer the local Indians. Eventually, the city had to be abandoned because of continuing battles with the Pueblo Indians. The Spanish retook the region in 1692.

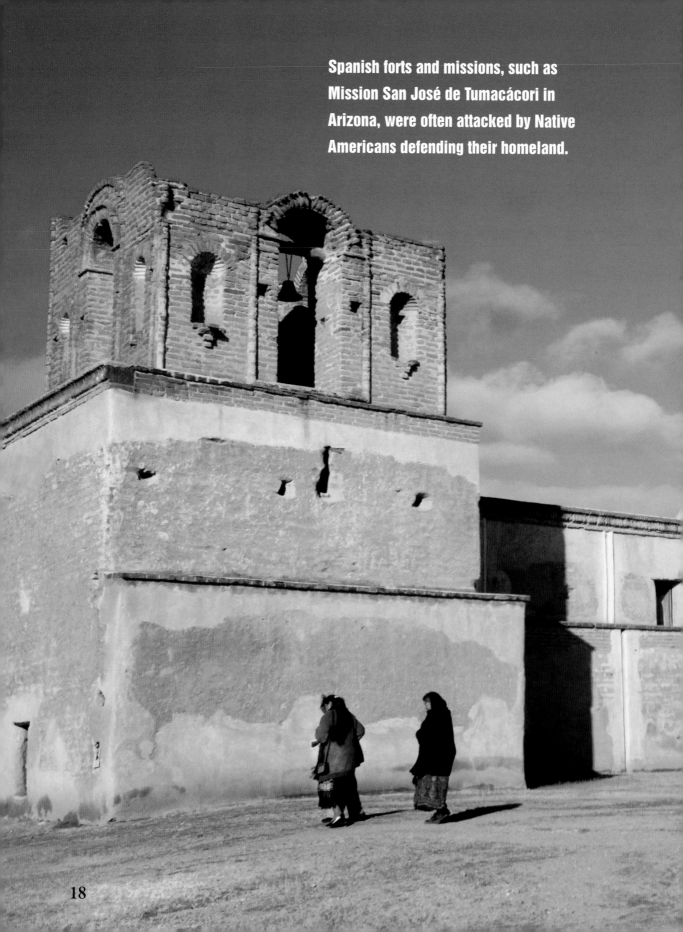

Spanish forts and missions, such as Mission San José de Tumacácori in Arizona, were often attacked by Native Americans defending their homeland.

The Spanish were slow to move into Arizona because Apache Indians aggressively defended their homeland. In the mid-1700s, Spanish miners moved in with the discovery of silver. Missionaries slowly filtered into the area, and ranches began to appear. Spanish forts, called presidios, sprang up to help protect the colonists from attacks by Native Americans.

In 1821, Mexico won its independence from Spain, and so took control of large areas of the Southwest. After the end of the Mexican-American War in 1848, the United States took control of most of what is today Arizona and New Mexico. The United States bought the final southern part of Arizona and New Mexico in 1853, in a transaction called the Gadsden Purchase.

The United States bought the final southern part of Arizona and New Mexico in 1853.

Actors recreate the 1836 attack by Mexican forces on the Alamo, a fort in modern-day San Antonio, Texas. On March 6, 1836, most of the Alamo's defenders were killed. However, Texas forces defeated the Mexican army a few weeks later.

TEXAS

The Spanish were slow to settle the area known today as Texas. A few expeditions explored parts of Texas, but they didn't make a big effort to colonize. It was only after a French expedition in 1685 that the Spanish decided to colonize it before someone else did.

Over the next six years, a number of missions were started, but most failed because of poor relations with Native Americans. Finally, the Spanish built a fort on the eastern side of Texas to serve as a buffer between the French in Louisiana and the Spanish in Mexico City. The Spanish built a number of missions on the east side of Texas.

When Mexico won its independence from Spain in 1821, it gained control of Texas. By 1836, Texans had declared their independence from Mexico. They formed an independent territory called the Republic of Texas. In 1845, Texas joined the United States as the 28th state.

CALIFORNIA

After seeing the wealth of the Aztecs, the Spanish were anxious to find other civilizations that were rich with gold and treasure. They also wanted to find a quick route to Asia, a water passage through the New World from the Atlantic Ocean to the Pacific Ocean.

In the early 1540s, conquistador Juan Rodríguez Cabrillo led three ships to explore the California coast. In 1543, after the accidental death of Cabrillo, the ships headed back to the Atlantic Ocean. They had failed to find gold or a water route connecting the oceans. Spain temporarily lost interest in California.

Juan Rodríguez Cabrillo was the first European to visit California. He claimed the area for Spain in 1542.

Explorer Francis Drake claimed California for England in 1579. This gave the Spanish the motivation they needed to continue exploring the western edge of North America.

In 1602, Spanish explorer Sebastián Vizcaíno mapped the coast of California from San Diego to Monterey Bay. The Spanish claimed to own Southern California, and the English claimed Northern California. The French and the Russians also wanted to claim these areas. Of course, these claims were made without talking to the Native American nations who already lived there. However, California was far away from the European countries. It was difficult, dangerous, and expensive to settle in California, and so settlement was slow.

The Spanish constructed missions in Baja California (now part of Mexico) in the 1690s. In the 1760s, missions were started in San Diego, California, and farther north. After that, the Spanish royalty permitted people to settle on large ranches. They believed that the best way to enforce their claim on the land was by having Spanish people actually live there.

The Spanish continued their colonization of the land until 1821, when Mexico won its independence. In 1848, Mexico gave California to the United States at the end of the Mexican-American War. In 1849, with the discovery of gold, California went on the fast track to statehood.

A group of vaqueros, or cowboys, outside the Santa Inéz Mission in California. The mission, founded in 1804, is the 19th of 21 missions built by Franciscan priests from 1769 to 1823.

25

SPANISH SETTLEMENT OF OTHER AREAS

The Spanish attempted to colonize most of the land that is today's southern border of the United States. California, Arizona, New Mexico, Texas, and Florida were their main North American colonies. They also tried to colonize parts of modern-day Louisiana, although the French had a better foothold there. The Spanish explored as far north as Kansas, possibly even taking a small expedition into Nebraska, although their claims there never took hold. The French had laid claim to the Mississippi River and the nearby territories.

In 1541, Spanish explorer Hernando de Soto crossed the Mississippi River near today's city of Memphis, Tennessee. He sought gold and jewels.

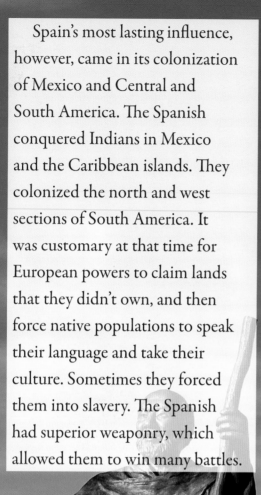

Spain's most lasting influence, however, came in its colonization of Mexico and Central and South America. The Spanish conquered Indians in Mexico and the Caribbean islands. They colonized the north and west sections of South America. It was customary at that time for European powers to claim lands that they didn't own, and then force native populations to speak their language and take their culture. Sometimes they forced them into slavery. The Spanish had superior weaponry, which allowed them to win many battles.

But the deadliest Spanish weapons were diseases, such as smallpox, brought from Europe. The native populations had no immunity to the diseases. Their populations were decimated all across North and South America.

As Spanish and Indian populations mingled and intermarried, they produced a new generation of mixed ancestry. This new generation of people would soon declare their independence from Spain. These people would later be known as Hispanic and Latino, and would become powerful leaders, educators, and scientists in the New World.

A sculpture in Albuquerque, New Mexico, shows the Spanish exploration of many areas of today's United States.

GLOSSARY

ANCESTORS

The people from whom a person is directly descended. Usually this term refers to people in generations prior to a person's grandparents.

AZTEC

A powerful civilization in southern Mexico, emerging in the 1300s. The Aztec civilization came to an end in 1521 at the hands of Spanish conquistadors.

CARIBBEAN

The islands and area of the Caribbean Sea, roughly the area between Florida and South and Central America.

CONQUISTADORS

Spanish military men who explored the New World and conquered many of the Indian tribes living in the Americas.

GADSDEN PURCHASE

The United States bought southern Arizona and southwest New Mexico in 1853 (ratified by Congress in 1854) in a transaction called the Gadsden Purchase.

HISPANIOLA

A large island in the Caribbean Sea. Today it is split into two countries, Haiti and the Dominican Republic.

IMMUNITY

The human immune system "remembers" when viruses or bacteria attack the body. From then on, the immune system can kill the germs quickly.

Without immunity, people often die. Natives in the Americas had a lack of immunity against the European disease of smallpox. Many thousands of people died.

INCA
A civilization on the west side of South America. They emerged in the 1200s and were conquered by the Spanish in the 1530s.

MAYA
A civilization in Central America that existed from about 200 AD to about 900 AD.

MEXICAN-AMERICAN WAR
In 1845, the independent Republic of Texas became a part of the United States. This angered Mexico, which considered Texas a part of its territory. The United States and Mexico also clashed over control of California. These conflicts led to war between the two countries, which lasted from 1846 until 1848.

NEW WORLD
The areas of North, Central, and South America, as well as islands near these land masses. The term was often used by European explorers.

NORTHWEST PASSAGE
A water passage that Europeans hoped to find that linked the Atlantic Ocean to the Pacific Ocean.

SMALLPOX
An often-deadly disease unknowingly brought by the Spanish to the Americas. The native peoples had no immunity to smallpox, so it spread like wildfire throughout their populations.

INDEX

A

Americas (*see also* Central America, North America, and South America) 4, 8
Apache nation 19
Arizona 8, 15, 17, 19, 26
Asia 4, 11, 22
Atlantic Ocean 4, 22
Aztecs 17, 22

B

Bahamas 11
Baja California 24

C

Cabeza de Vaca, Álvar Núñez 15
Cabrillo, Juan Rodríguez 22
California 8, 22, 24, 26
California, Northern 24
California, Southern 24
Caribbean islands 4, 8, 28
Catholic 6
Central America 8, 28
Colorado River 17
Columbus, Christopher 4, 11
Coronado, Francisco Vásquez de 17
Cuba 11, 12

D

Dominican Republic 11
Drake, Francis 24

E

Easter 12
England 24
Europe 4, 28

F

Festival of Flowers, The 12
Florida 8, 12, 14, 15, 26
France 14, 15

G

Gadsden Purchase 19
Grand Canyon 17

H

Haiti 11
Hispaniola 11

I

Incas 17

J

Jamestown, VA

K

Kansas 17, 26
King of Spain 14

L

Los Angeles, CA 8
Louisiana 21, 26

M

Menéndez de Avilés, Pedro 14
Mexican-American War 19, 24
Mexico 19, 21, 24, 28
Mexico City 15, 21
Mississippi 15
Mississippi River 26
Monterey Bay 24

N

Nárvaez, Pánfilo de 15
Nebraska 26
New Mexico 8, 15, 17, 19, 26

New World 4, 6, 11, 22, 28
North America 24, 28
Northwest Passage 4

O

Oñate, Don Juan de 17

P

Pacific Ocean 4, 15, 22
Panama Canal 4
Pascua Florida (*see also* Festival of Flowers, The) 12
Ponce de León, Juan 12
Pueblo Indians 17
Puerto Rico 11

R

Republic of Texas 21

S

Samana Cay 11
San Antonio, TX 8
San Diego, CA 24
San Salvador 11
Santa Fe, NM 8, 17
Seven Cities of Gold 17
South America 8, 28
Spain 4, 12, 15, 17, 19, 21, 22, 28
St. Augustine, FL 14

T

Tampa Bay, FL 15
Texas 8, 15, 17, 21, 26

U

United States 14, 19, 21, 24, 26

V

Virginia 14
Vizcaíno, Sebastián 24